After an embarrassing moment at school, Pancake Junior, or PJ for short, learns he needs glasses. Join PJ on a fun trip to the eye doctor and realize how much better he can see - and read - with glasses.

Rachael has been a middle school teacher, park ranger, cat mom, and ADHD life navigator. She's hiked the tallest mountain in Wyoming, despite getting lost in her own backyard. Her first book is based on her own experience needing glasses - created with the help of her students. Look out for her upcoming books to see her quirky characters navigate life's weirdly typical experiences.

Website: weirdlytypicalworks.com
Instagram: weirdlytypicalworks

PJ's First Pair of Glasses

By Rachael Esh

PJ's First Pair of Glasses by Rachael Esh
Publisher: Weirdly Typical Works

Website: weirdlytypicalworks.com
Instagram: weirdlytypicalworks

No part of this publication may be reproduced in whole or in part, or stored in a retrieval system, or transmitted in any form or by any means, electronic, mechanical, photocopying, recording, or otherwise, without written permission of the publisher/author. For information regarding permission please write to weirdlytypicalworks@gmail.com

ISBN: 978-0-578-29680-7

Text and illustration copyright © 2022 Rachael Esh

Dedication

To each and every one of my students over the years. Thank you for your encouragement and inspiration.

Dear Readers,

Thank you for purchasing my very first book. I wrote this book for every little kid who needs glasses. If you enjoy this read, it would mean the world to me if you could leave a kind review on Amazon. Your feedback will help me continue my dream of writing and illustrating children's books for kids and families all over the world.

Today wasn't just any school day. Today was *special*.

Pancake Junior - PJ to his friends - could not wait to present his favorite book for show and tell.

He *loved* to read.

PJ wanted to look his best for school.

So he put on his favorite cowboy outfit,
high-fived himself in the mirror,
and brushed his teeth *extra* well.

When show and tell began that day, the teacher asked PJ to read the instructions on the front board.

But no matter how hard he squinted, the words were just a blur.

One student snickered,

"He can't even read!"

PJ's face flushed as red as strawberry jam.

He was so embarrassed that he refused to present his book for show and tell or talk to anyone for the rest of the day.

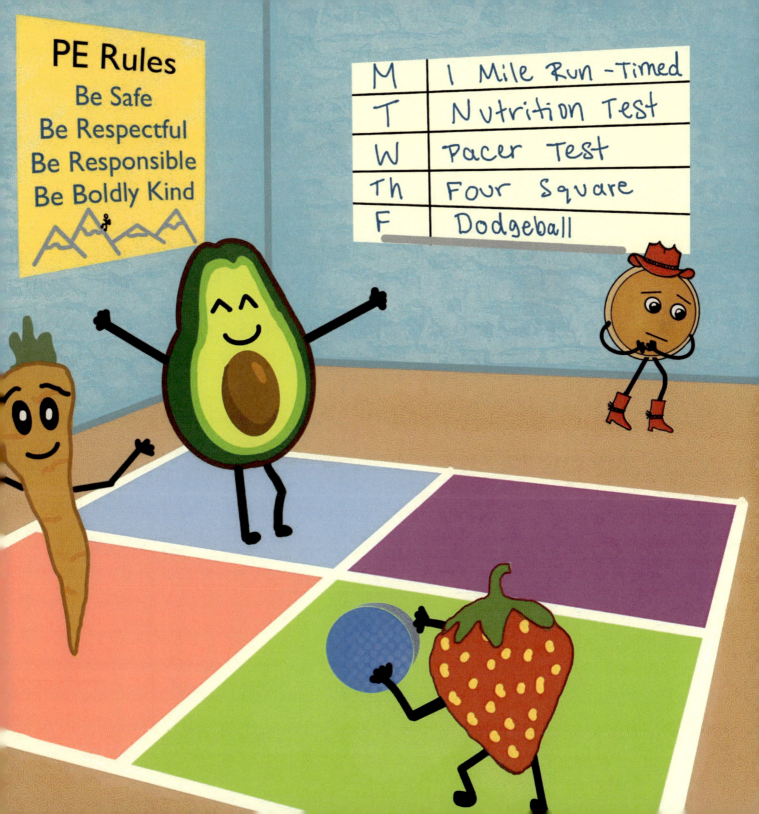

At home, his father knocked on PJ's door and asked if his homework was done.

"Why should I bother? All the kids think I'm stupid."

Pancake Senior sat next to PJ and asked what happened.

PJ told his story, waiting for his father's disappointment. Instead, his father asked PJ to read a word on his poster.

"Son, can you tell me what this says?"

But just like at school, the words were a blur.
"PJ, it seems like you need glasses."

"Glasses? But I'm only in 2nd grade!"

"I got my first pair of glasses when I was your age. This happens to a lot of kids."

"Oh. I guess that's true."

The next day, Dad took PJ to the eye doctor.

He was a little nervous, but it turned out to be fun!

He looked through big machines and saw different shapes and colors.

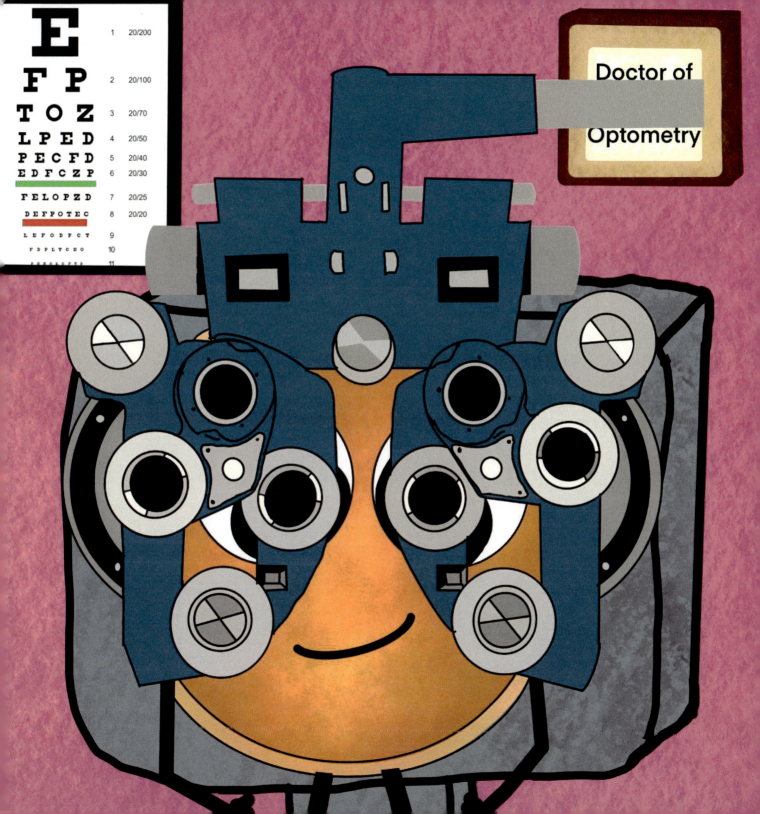

He got to twirl in a swivel chair and look at letters.

"Wheeeee!"

He even got a cherry lollipop. His favorite!

Dr. Croissant explained that PJ had nearsighted vision.

"You can see objects up close, but things far away are blurry."

She handed PJ the glasses he got to pick off the big wall.

"Now see if you can read the words on the chalkboard at school tomorrow."

Outside, PJ couldn't believe his eyes. He saw things he had never seen before!

He saw crisp, green leaves.

He saw feathers on birds, street signs,

and an ice cream cone in the clouds.

Going back to school was a little scary. PJ thought kids might make fun of him, but he decided it didn't matter.

He loved his new red glasses.

And finally, when it was time for show and tell, PJ proudly read the rules and strolled to the front on the class to tell everyone about his favorite book.

Made in the USA
Las Vegas, NV
13 May 2024

89876413R00021